SCHIRMER'S LIBRARY
OF MUSICAL CLASSICS

T0039745

PIANO MASTERWORKS

EARLY ADVANCED LEVEL

54 Pieces by 21 Composers

ISBN 978-1-4950-0691-3

G. SCHIRMER, *Inc.*

DISTRIBUTED BY

HAL•LEONARD®
CORPORATION
7777 W. BLUEMOUND RD. P.O. BOX 13819 MILWAUKEE, WI 53213

www.musicsalesclassical.com
www.halleonard.com

CONTENTS

FRÉDÉRIC CHOPIN

FRANÇOIS COUPERIN

CLAUDE DEBUSSY

ANTONÍN DVOŘÁK

JOHN FIELD

CHARLES T. GRIFFES

EDVARD GRIEG

FRANZ LISZT

FELIX MENDELSSOHN

(Continued on next page)

España

Preludio

Isaac Albéniz
Op. 165

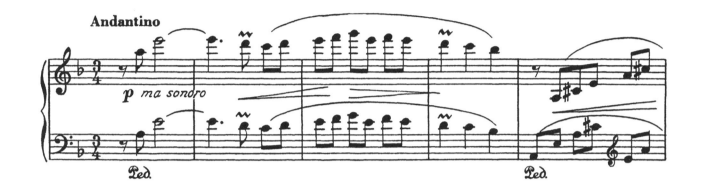

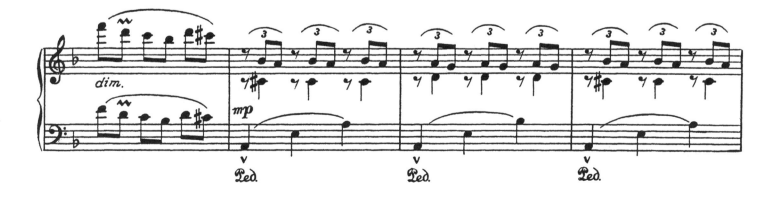

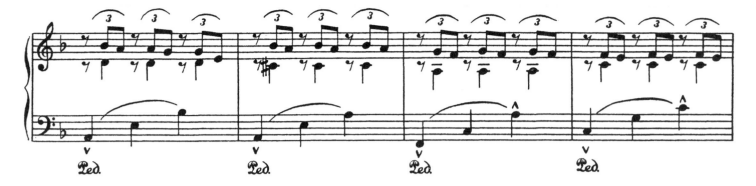

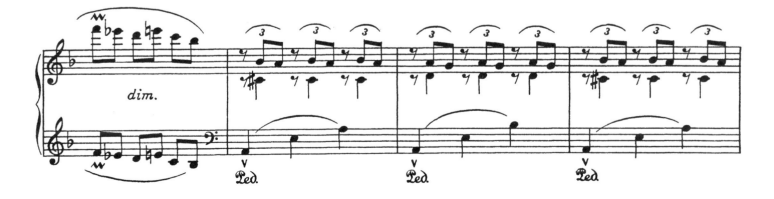

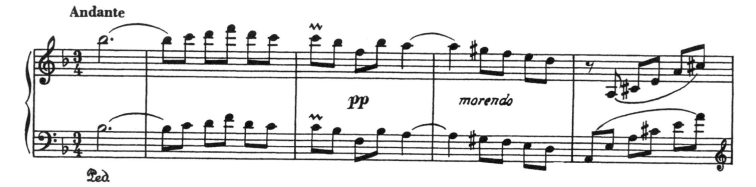

Tango

Malagueña

13

14

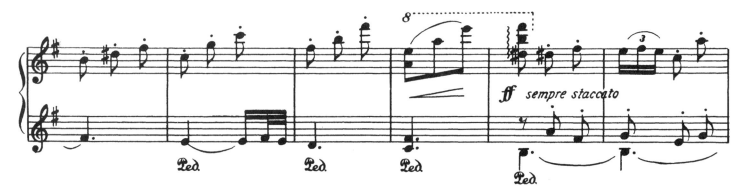

Sinfonia No. 2
in C minor

Johann Sebastian Bach
BWV 788

Allegro vivace (♩. = 100)

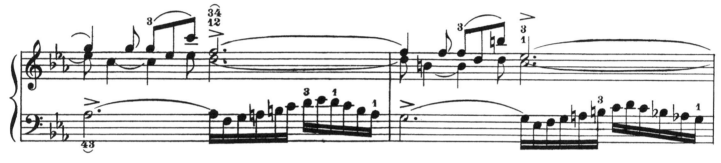

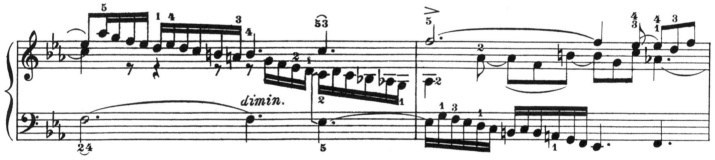

Sinfonia No. 15
in B minor

Johann Sebastian Bach

BWV 801

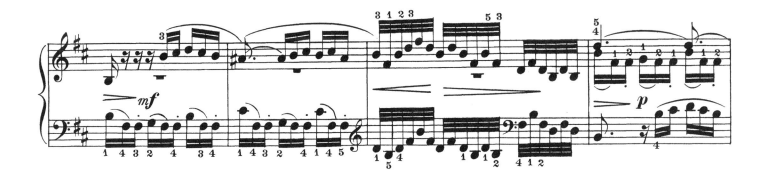

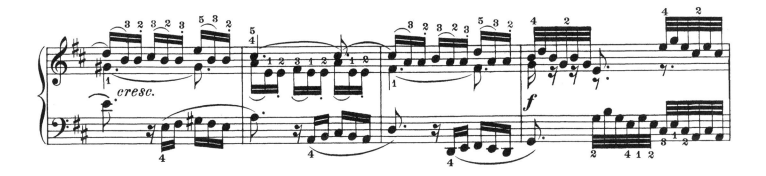

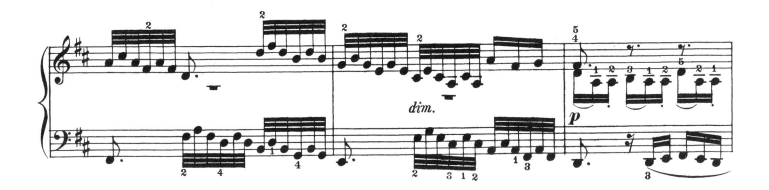

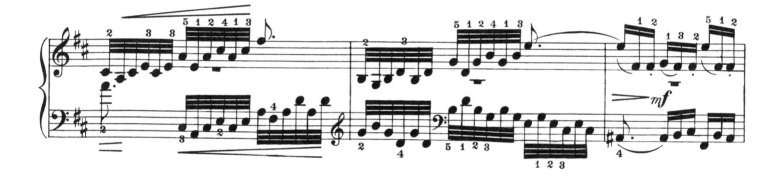

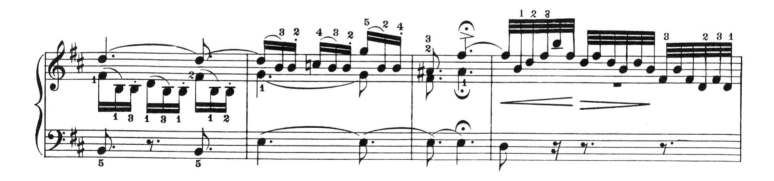

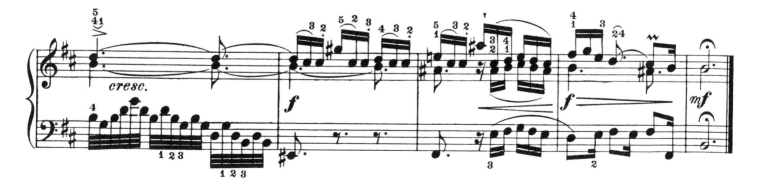

Prelude and Fughetta
in D minor

Johann Sebastian Bach
BWV 899

Prelude
Sostenuto

Fughetta
Andante

Prelude and Fughetta
in G Major

Johann Sebastian Bach
BWV 902

Prelude

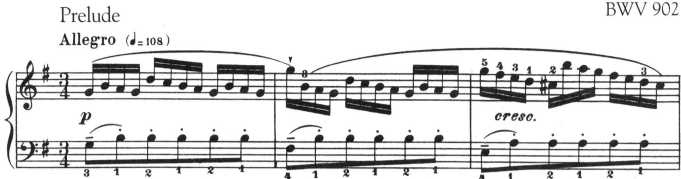

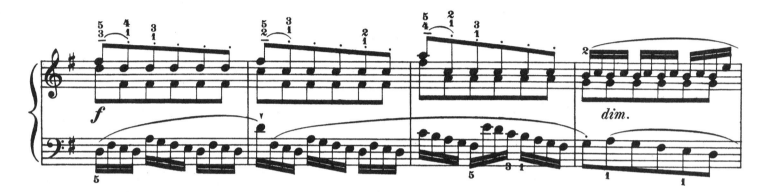

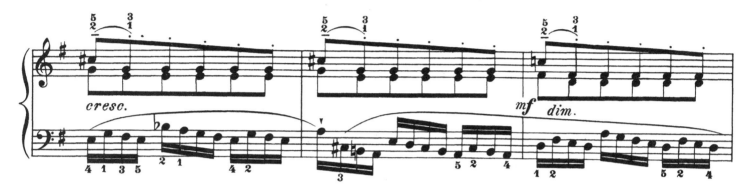

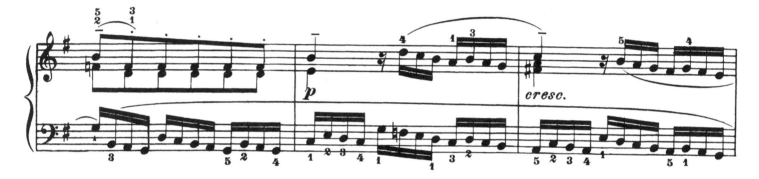

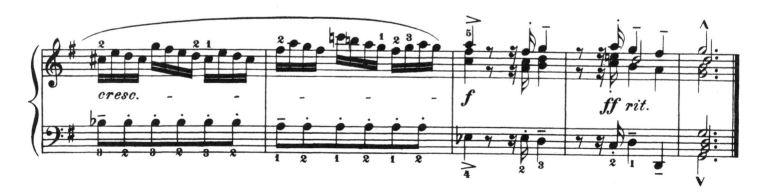

24

Fugehetta
Allegretto (♪=176)

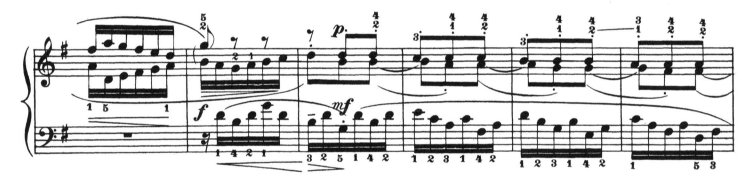

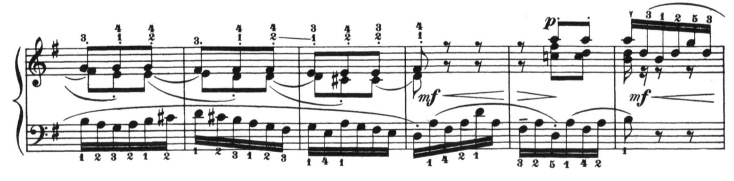

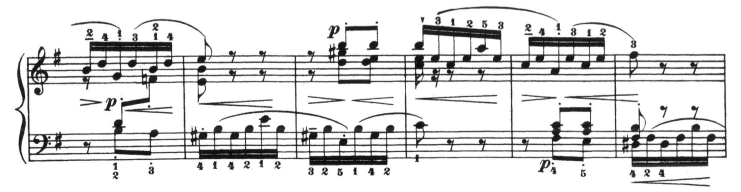

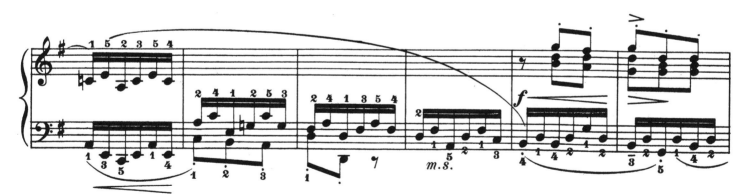

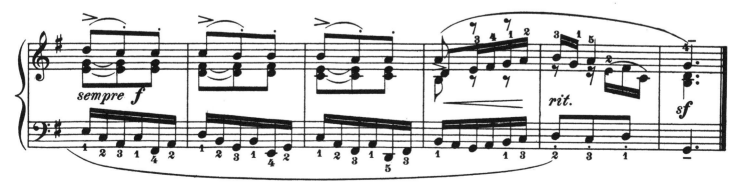

Fugue
in C Major

Johann Sebastian Bach
BWV 953

Allegro

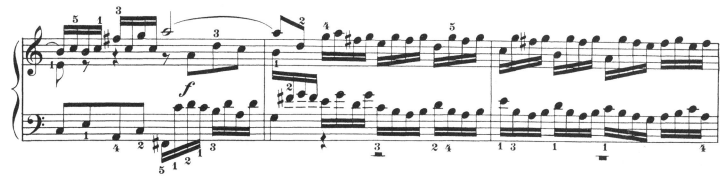

Fugue
in C minor

Johann Sebastian Bach
BWV 961

Allegro

a.) etc.

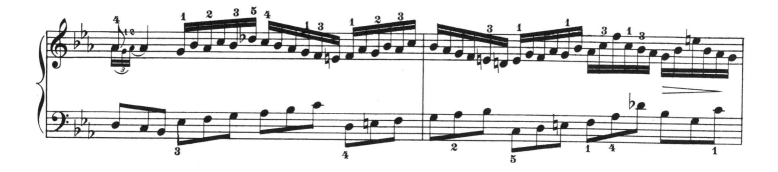

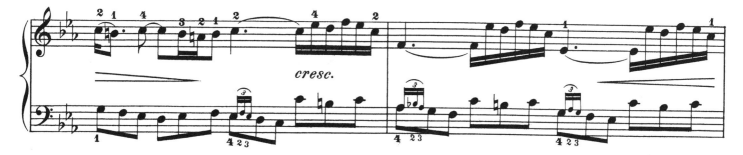

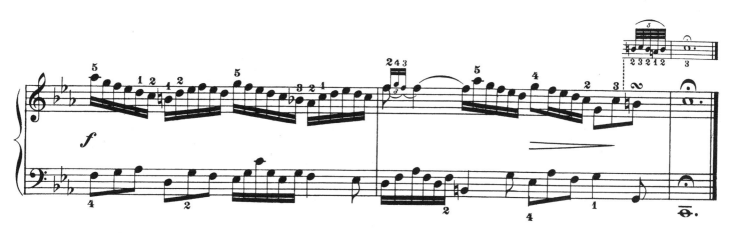

Prelude and Fughetta
in E minor

Johann Sebastian Bach
BWV 900

Prelude
Andantino

Fughetta
Moderato

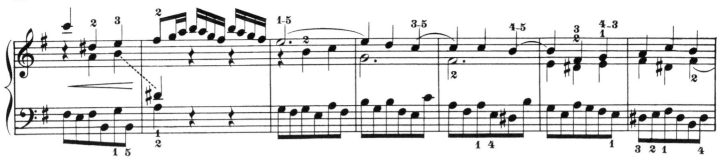

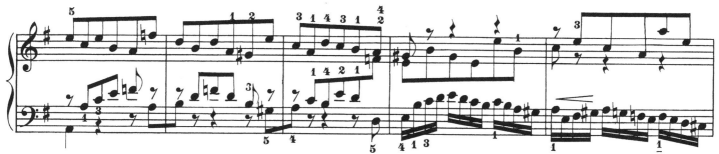

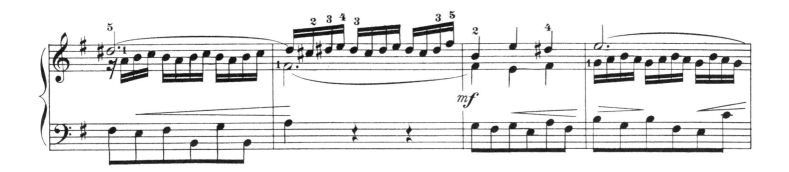

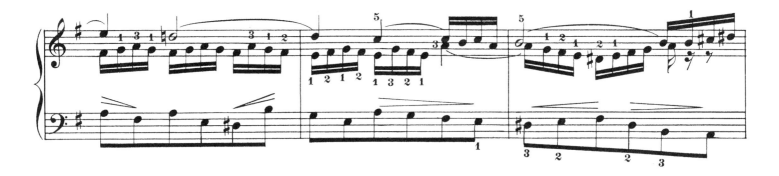

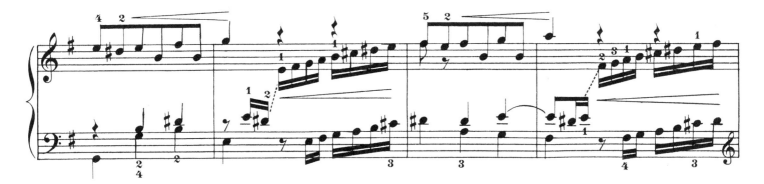

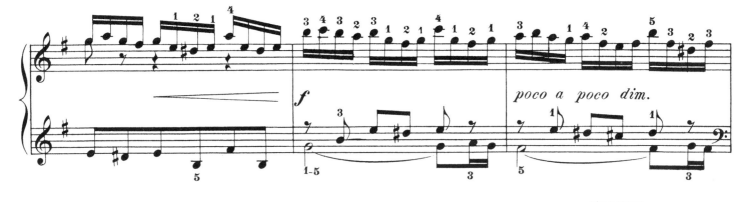

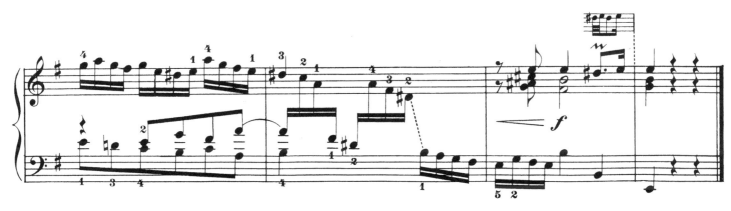

Allegro barbaro

Tempo giusto (♩ = 76 – 84)

Béla Bartók

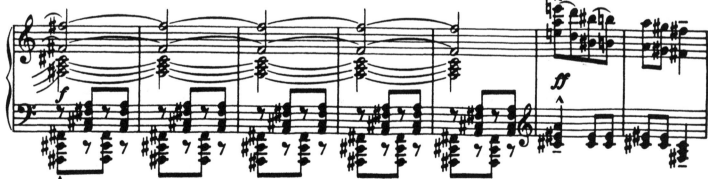

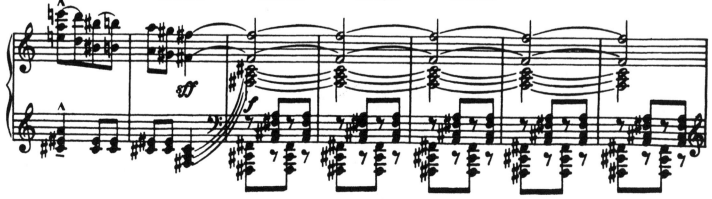

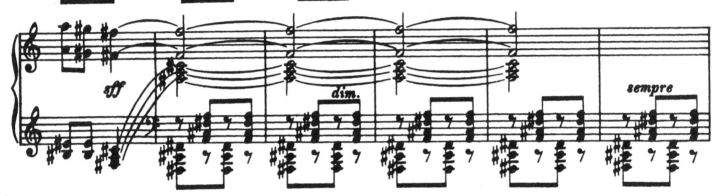

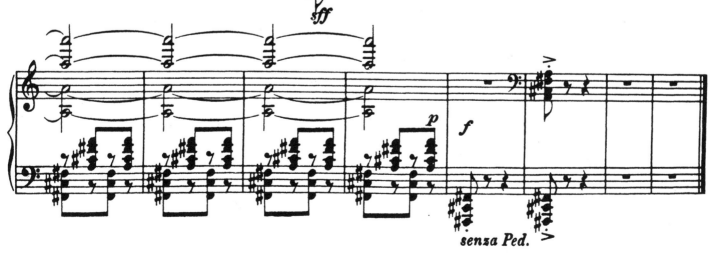

Andante cantabile

from Piano Sonata in C minor, "Pathétique"

Ludwig van Beethoven
Op. 13

a) To the best of our knowledge no one has yet remarked the striking affinity of the theme of this movement, even with reference to its external melodic structure, to that of one of the loftiest *Adagios* of grandest scope from the Master's last period;— we mean the *Adagio* of the Ninth Symphony, written almost a quarter of a century later. The performance of both demands an equally inspired mood. The player's task, to "make his fingers sing," may perhaps necessitate a more frequent use of the pedal than we have indicated, which must of course be controlled by a most watchful ear.

b) This first middle section of the Rondo (for such this *Adagio* is in form) may be taken slightly *meno andante,* i. e., slower; but no more so than needful (so as not to drag), and, therefore, in only a few places.

c) The turns in this and the next measure should not commence with, but immediately after, a sixteenth-note in the bass, thus: and:

a) A tasteful execution of this grace is impossible in strict time. An abbreviation of the first two principal notes (C and F♭) being quite as impracticable as a shifting of the inverted mordent into the preceding measure as an unaccented appoggiatura, the measure must simply be extended by an additional 32nd-note.

b) In this repetition of the theme, the left hand may be allowed to play a more expressive part; and, on the whole, a somewhat lighter shading of the melody is now admissible by way of contrast to the following (gloomier) middle section.

c) The ascending diminished fifth may be phrased, as it were, like a question, to which the succeeding bass figure may be regarded as the answer.

a) It appears advisable slightly to hasten this measure and the next, and then to retard the third not inconsiderably; the former on account of the cessation in the harmonic advance, the latter by reason of the varied modulation, which must be quite free from disquieting haste in its return to the theme.

b) Though strictly subordinated to the melody, the triplets should be brought out with animated distinctness.

c) The two 32nd-notes in the melody may very properly be sounded with the last note of the triplet of 16th-notes in the accompaniment; whereas a mathematically exact division would probably confuse both parts.

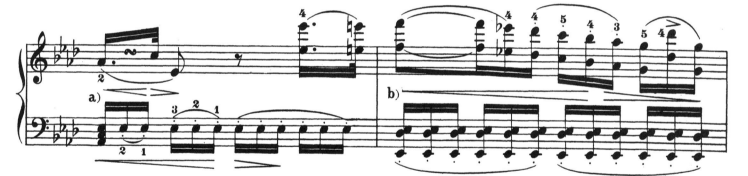

a) Execute like a triplet:

b) In the original, the shading of this passage is marked differently from that two measures before, the *diminuendo* already beginning with C, and not with A♭ as here marked. This latter nuance — the prolongation of the *crescendo* — appeals to our feeling as the more delicate, "more tenderly passionate," to quote Richard Wagner's happy remark on the "Interpretation of Beethoven."

c) Mark the separation of the slurs in this figure and those following; the six notes sound trivial if slurred together.

Adagio sostenuto

from Piano Sonata in C-sharp minor, "Moonlight"

Ludwig van Beethoven
Op. 27, No. 2

Abbreviations: M. T. signifies Main Theme; S. T., Sub-Theme; Cl. T., Closing Theme; D. G., Development-group; R., Return; Tr., Transition; Md. T., Mid-Theme; Ep., Episode.

a) It is evident that the highest part, as the melody, requires a firmer touch than the accompanying triplet-figure; and the first note in the latter must never produce the effect of a doubling of the melody in the lower octave.

b) A more frequent use of the pedal than is marked by the editor, and limited here to the most essential passages, is allowable; it is not advisable, however, to take the original directions *sempre senza sordini* (i. e., without dampers) too literally.

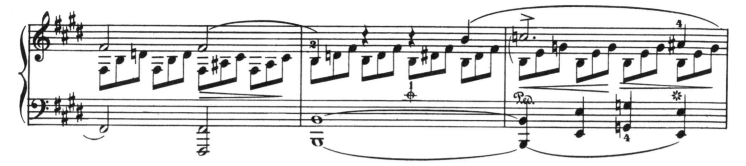

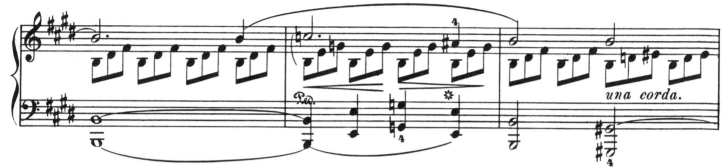

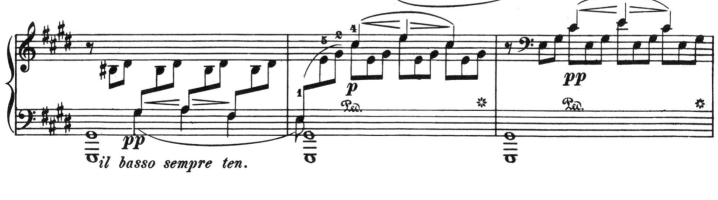

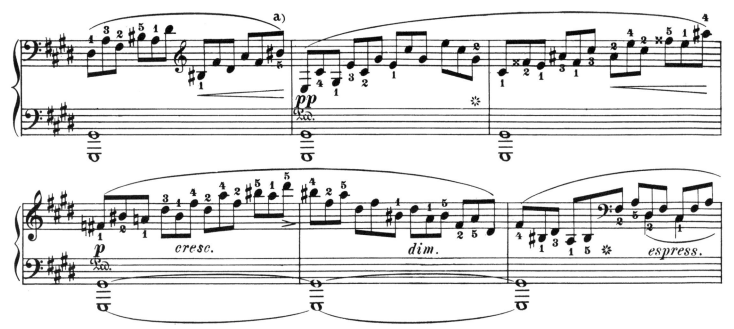

a) The player must guard against carrying his hand back with over-anxious haste. For, in any event, a strict pedantic observance of time is out of place in this period, which has rather the character of an improvisation.

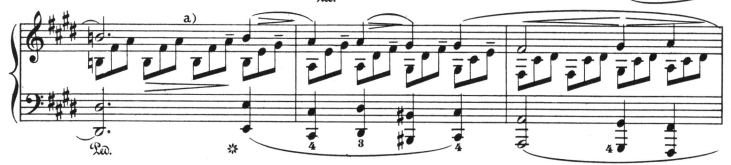

a) The notes with a dash above them may properly be dwelt upon in such a way as to give them the effect of suspensions, e. g., in fact, a utilization of the inner parts, in accordance with the laws of euphony and the course of the modulation, is recommended throughout the piece.

Rhapsody
in G minor

Johannes Brahms
Op. 79, No. 2

Molto passionato, ma non troppo allegro

Intermezzo

in A Major

from *Six Pieces for Piano*

Johannes Brahms
Op. 118, No. 2

Andante teneramente

Fantaisie-Impromptu
in C-sharp minor

Frédéric Chopin
Op. 66 (Posthumous)

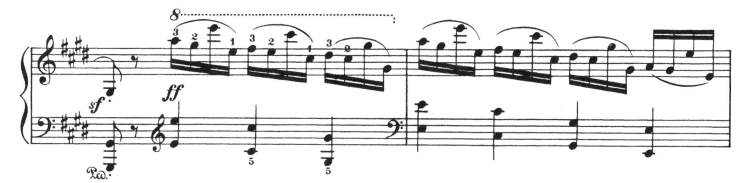

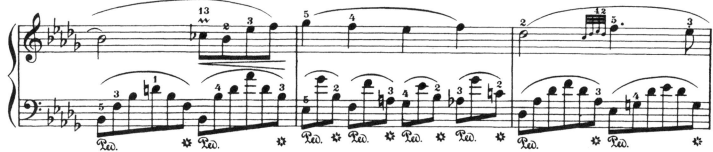

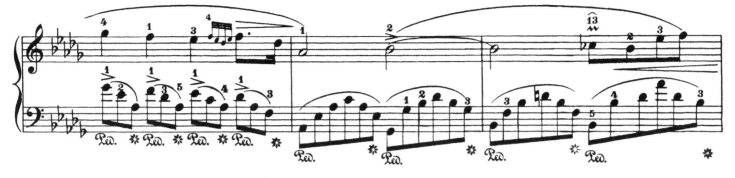

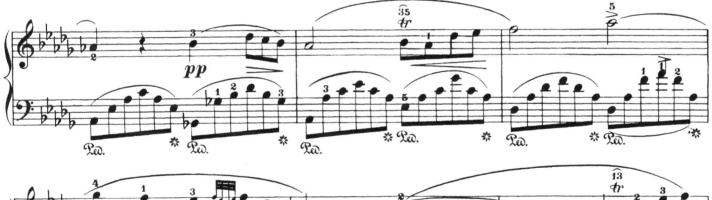

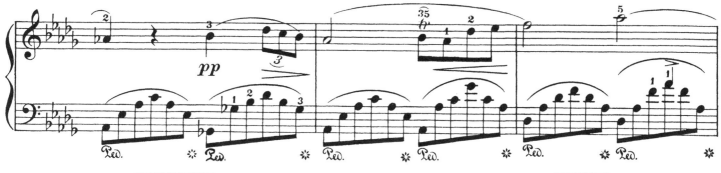

Tempo I° (Allegro agitato)

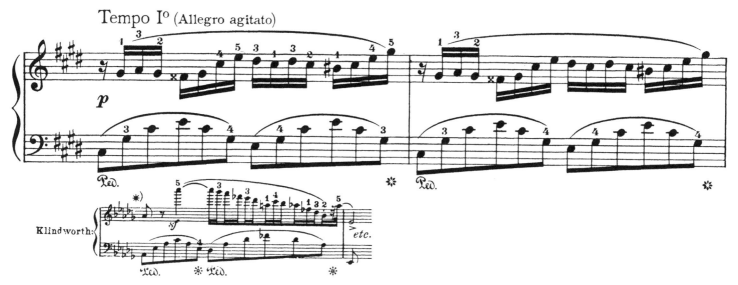

Klindworth:

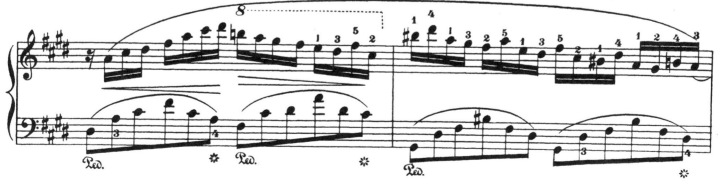

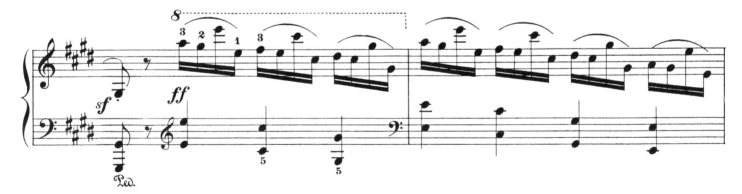

à Mademoiselle Lina Freppa

Mazurka
in A minor

Frédéric Chopin
Op. 17, No. 4

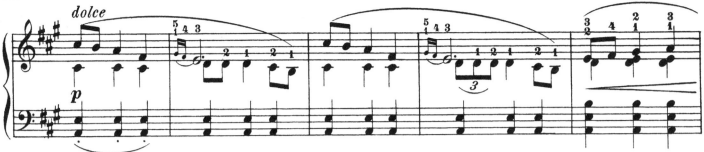

Nocturne
in E minor

Frédéric Chopin
Op. 72, No. 1
(Posthumous)

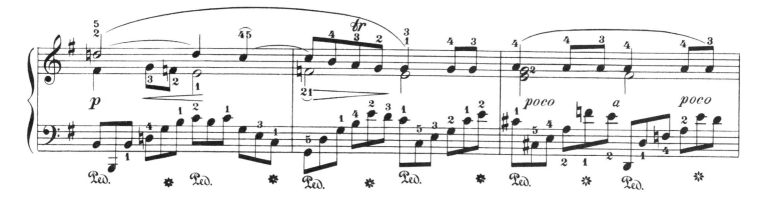

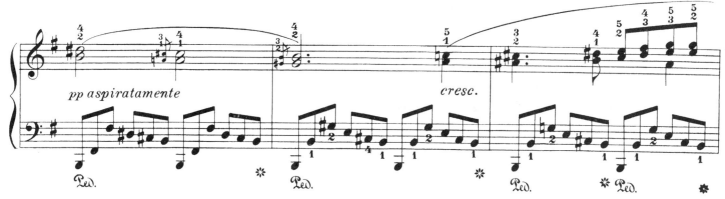

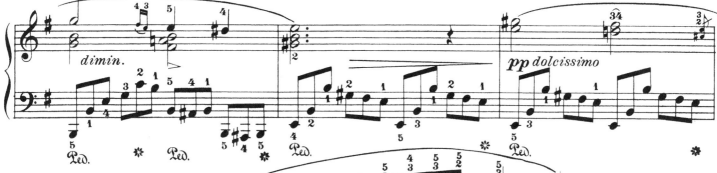

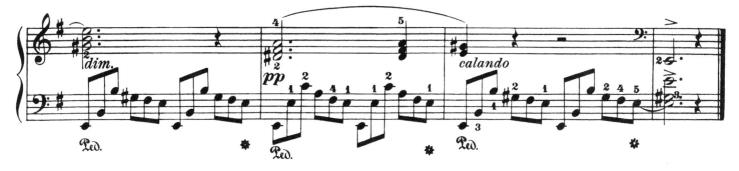

à Madame Camilla Pleyel

Nocturne
in E-flat Major

Frédéric Chopin
Op. 9, No. 2

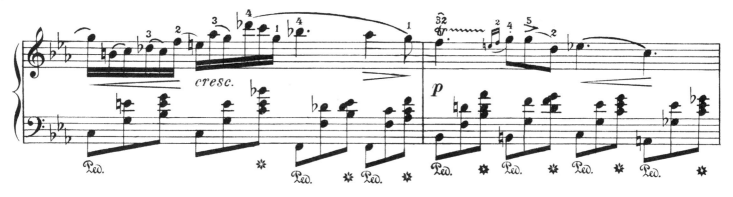

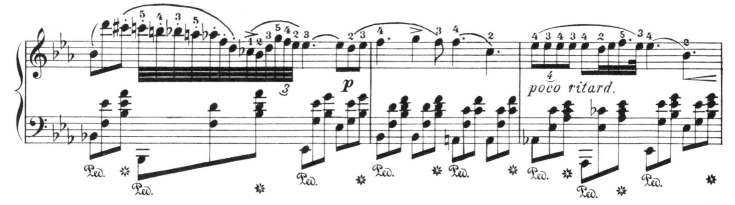

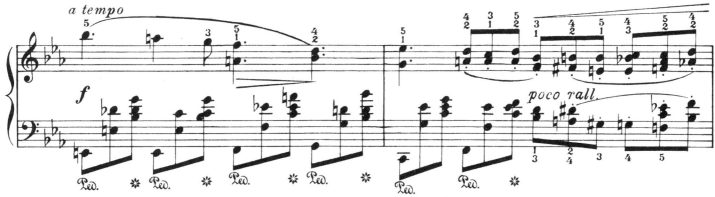

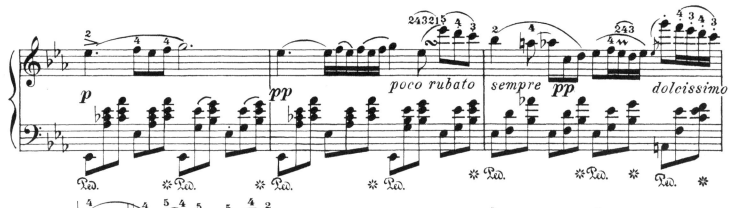

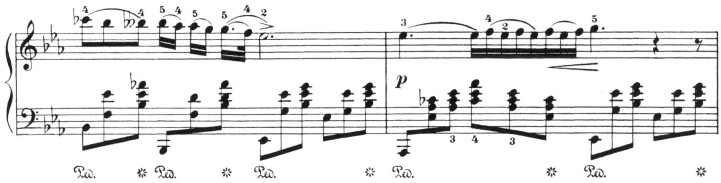

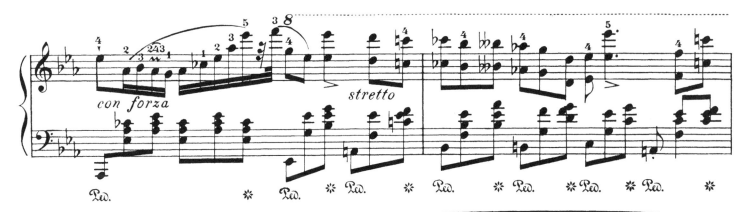

à Madame la Comtesse Delphine Potocka

Waltz
in D-flat Major
"Minute"

Frédéric Chopin
Op. 64, No. 1

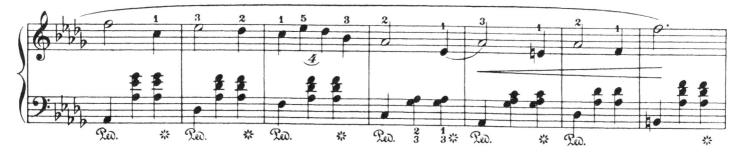

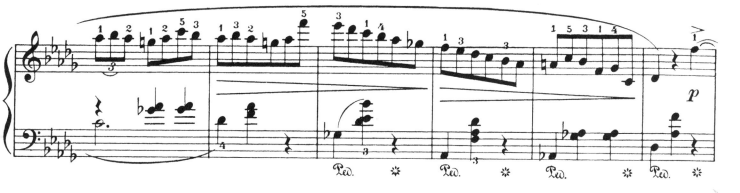

à Madame Nathaniel de Rothschild

Waltz

in C-sharp minor

Frédéric Chopin
Op. 64, No. 2

Più mosso

Più lento

Più mosso

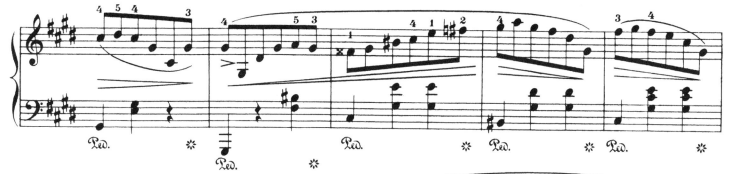

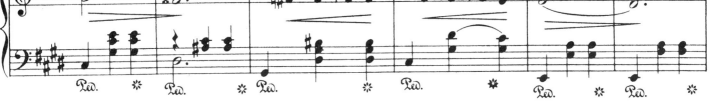

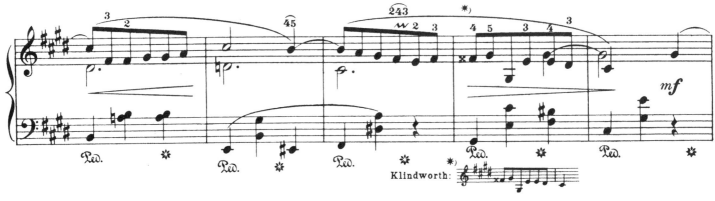

Klindworth:

Waltz
in A-flat Major

Frédéric Chopin
Op. 69, No. 1
(Posthumous)

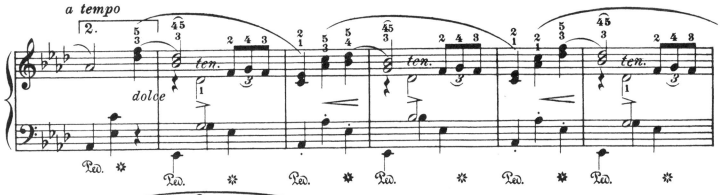

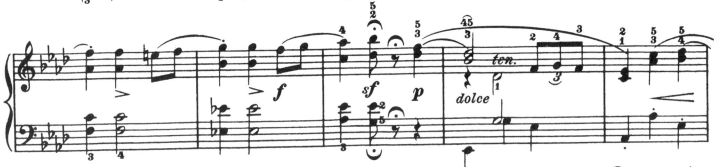

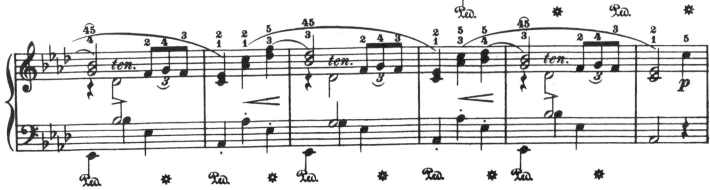

à M. Jules Fontana

Polonaise

in A Major
"Military"

Frédéric Chopin
Op. 40, No. 1

Allegro con brio

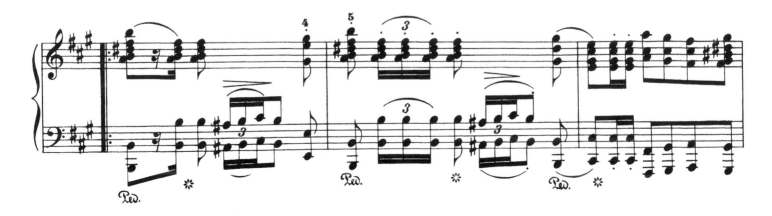

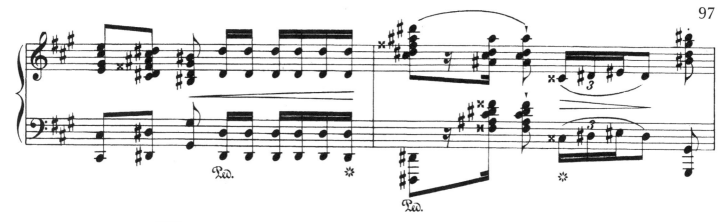

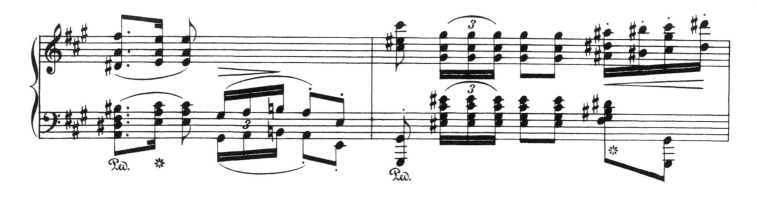

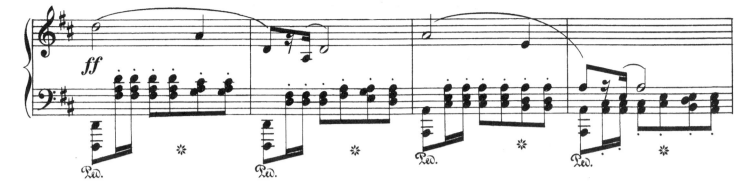

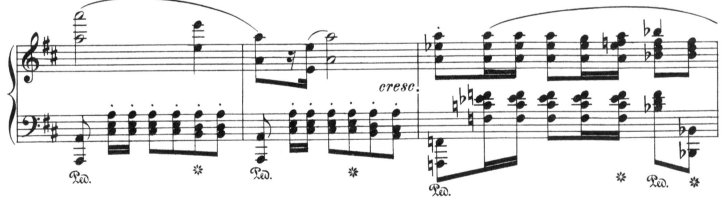

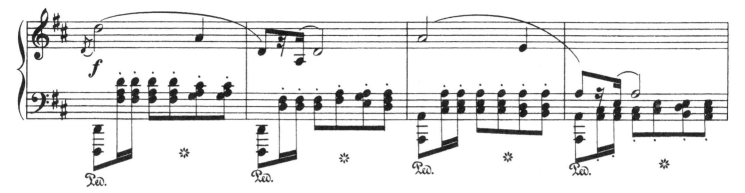

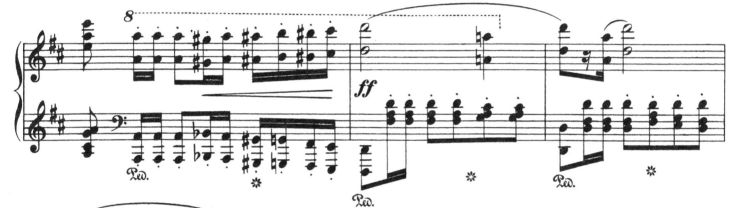

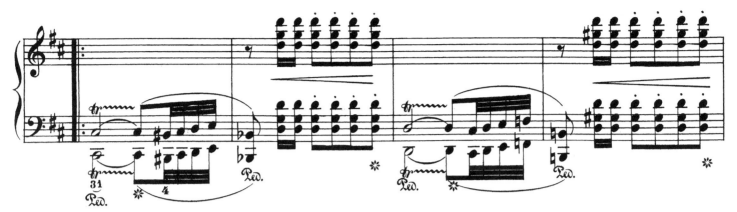

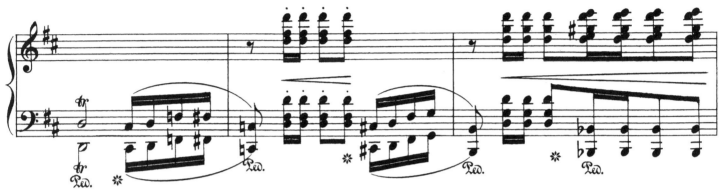

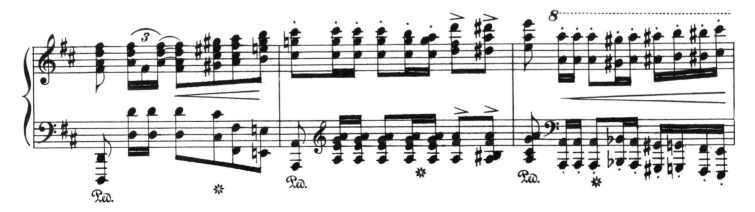

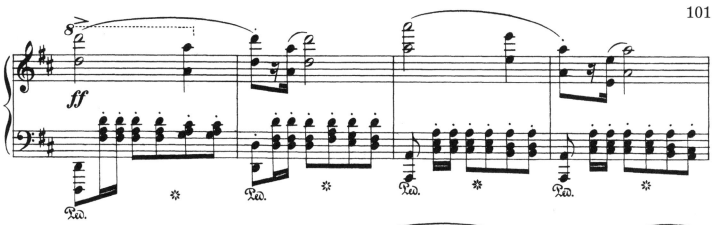

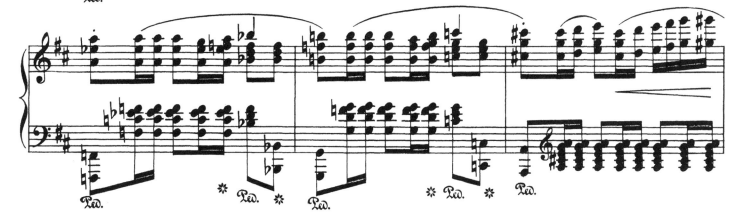

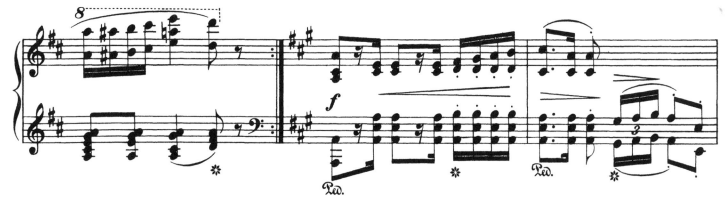

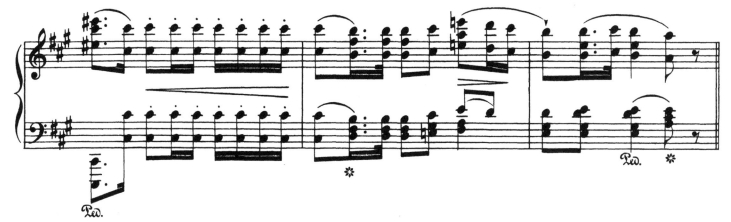

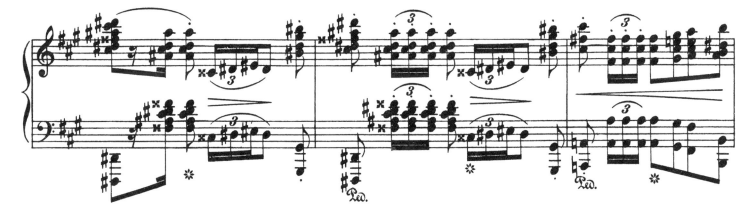

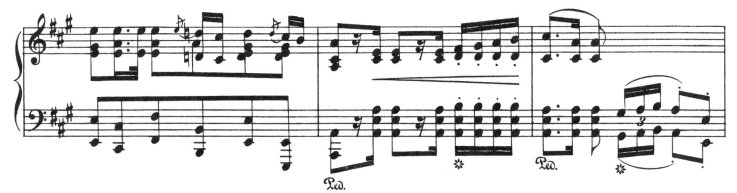

Le réveille-matin

from Suite No. 4 of *Harpsichord Pieces*, Book 1

François Couperin

* **May be omitted.**

104

La sérénade

(Serenade)

from *18 Characteristic Studies*

Johann Friedrich Burgmüller
Op. 109, No. 11

Allegretto grazioso (♪ = 176)

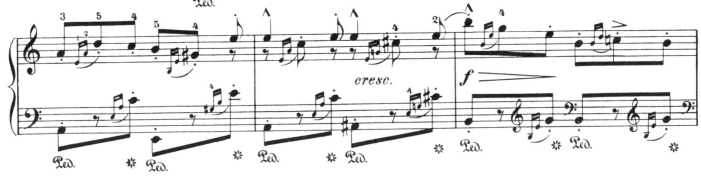

La réveil dans les bois

(Awakening in the Woods)
from *18 Characteristic Studies*

Johann Friedrich Burgmüller
Op. 109, No. 12

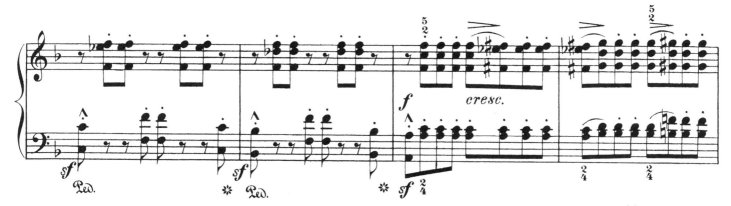

Clair de lune

from *Suite bergamasque*

Claude Debussy

Tempo rubato

pp

peu à peu cresc. et animé (louder and livelier)

r. h.

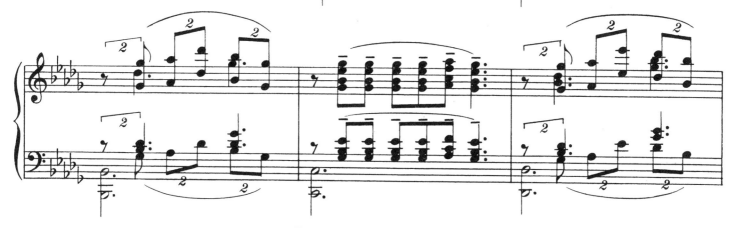

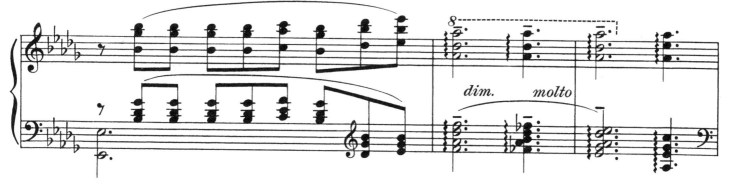

dim.   molto

un poco mosso

pp

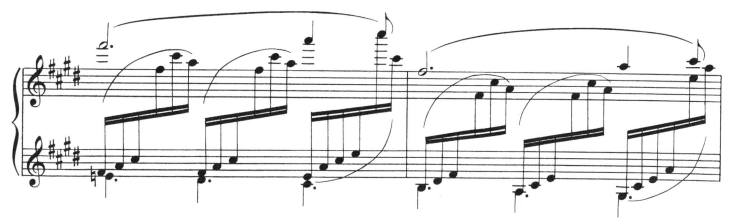

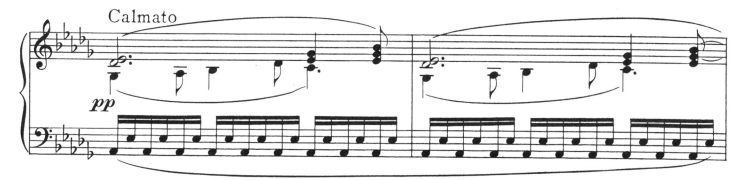

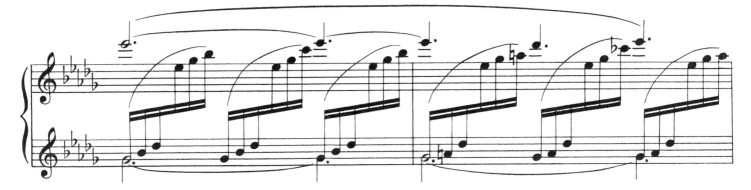

Tempo I

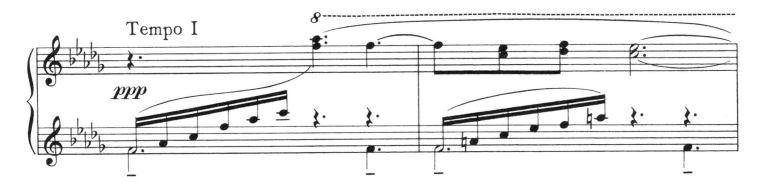

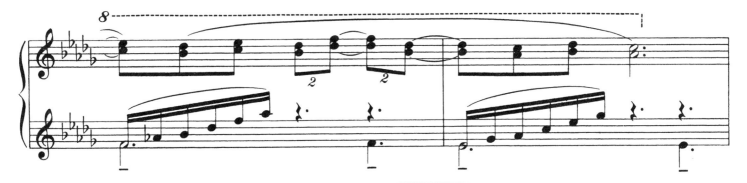

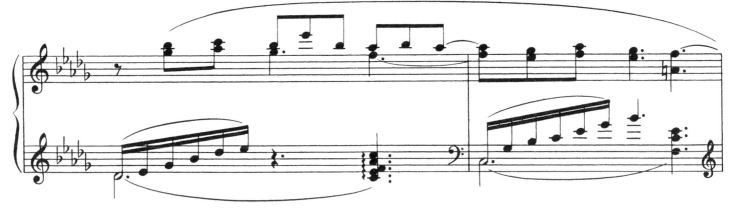

pp morendo jusqu'à la fin (more and more faint to the end)

Arabesque No. 2
from *Two Arabesques*

Claude Debussy

Allegretto scherzando

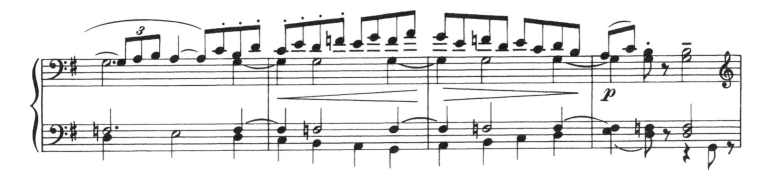

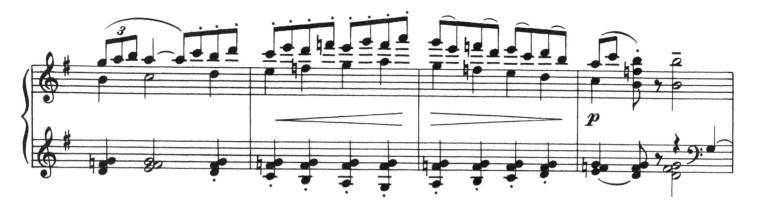

La cathédrale engloutie
from *Préludes*, Book 1

Claude Debussy

Profondément calme (Dans une brume doucement sonore)

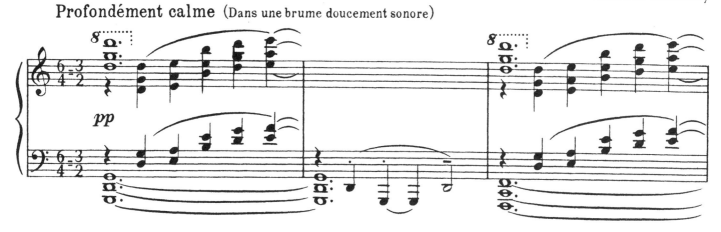

*) **Doux et fluide**

*)

*) Debussy, in his piano-roll recording (Welte-Mignon), played measures 7–12 and 22–83 in double speed.

Peu à peu sortant de la brume

Augmentez progressivement (Sans presser)

Sonore sans dureté

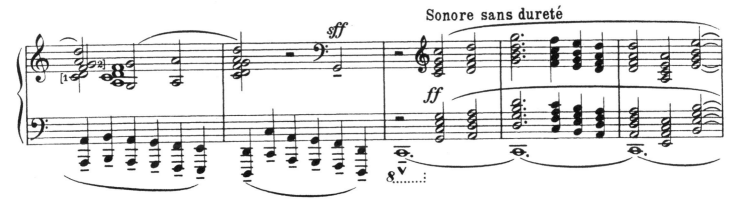

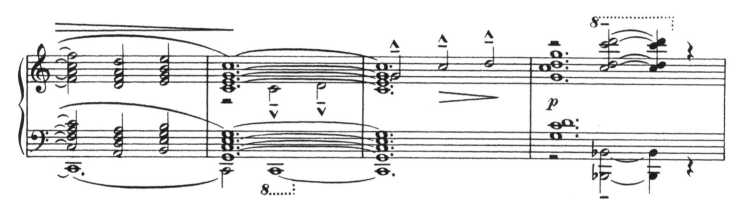

Un peu moins lent (Dans une expression allant grandissant)

pp expressif et concentré

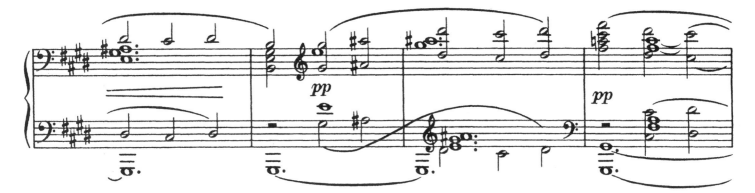

au Mouvement

pp Comme un écho de la phrase entendue pré-cédemment

Flottant et sourd

Dans la sonorité du début

pp

più pp

La fille aux cheveux de lin
from *Préludes*, Book 1

Claude Debussy

Très calme et doucement expressif (♩=66)

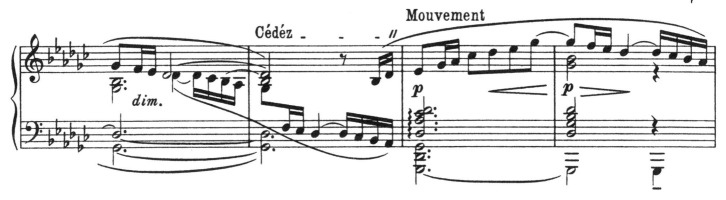

Cédéz _ _ // Mouvement (sans lourdeur)

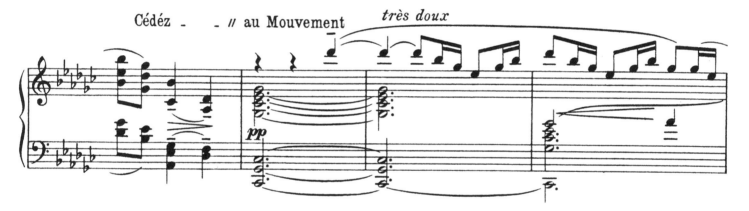

Cédéz _ _ // au Mouvement   *très doux*

Murmuré et en retenant peu à peu

Sarabande

from *Pour le piano*

Claude Debussy

Avec une elegance grave et lente (elegantly, solemnly and slowly)

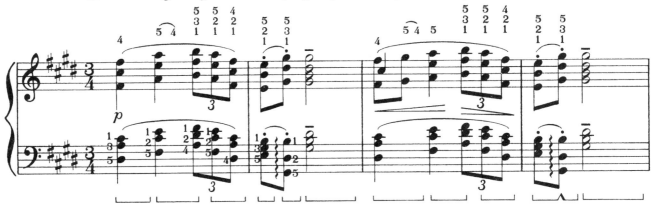

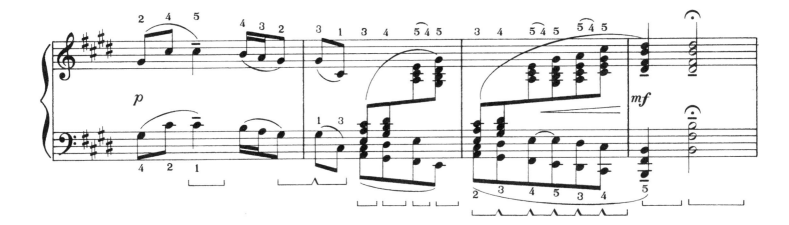

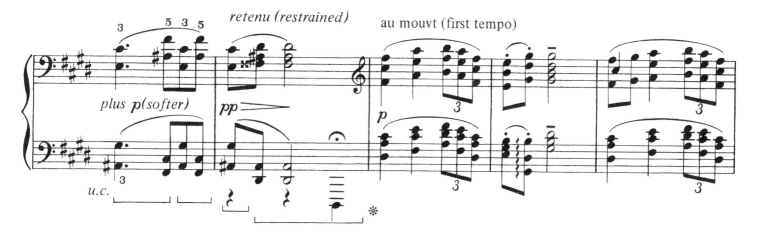

132

animez un peu (gradually faster)
très soutenu (very sustained)

au mouvt (first tempo)

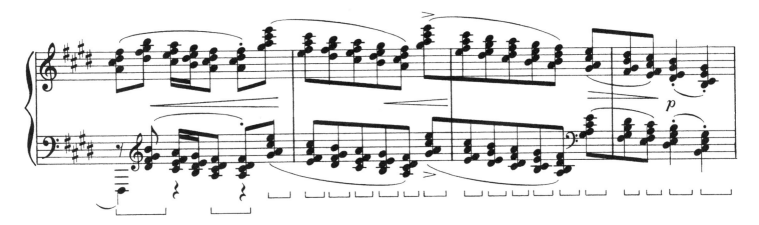

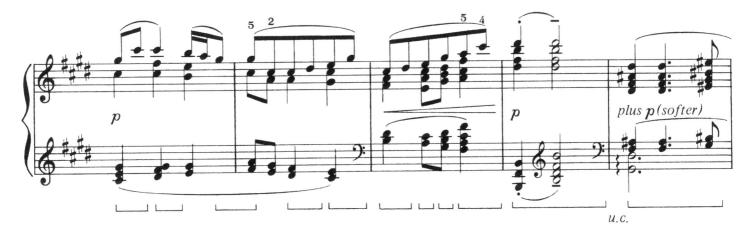

*plus **p** (softer)*

u.c.

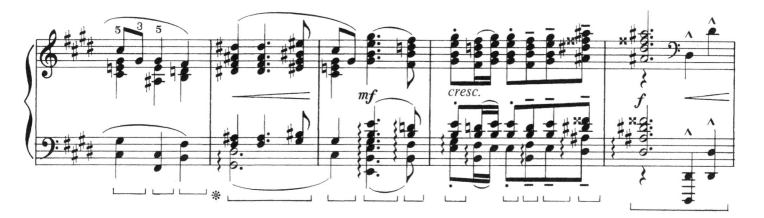

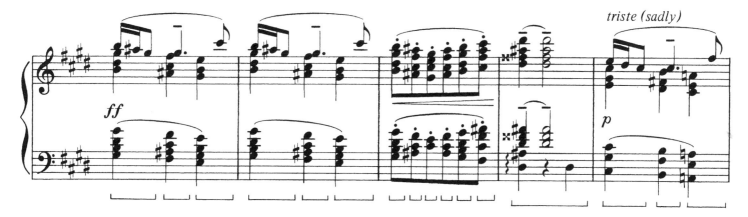

Poco lento e grazioso

from *Humoresques*

Antonín Dvořák
Op. 101, No. 7

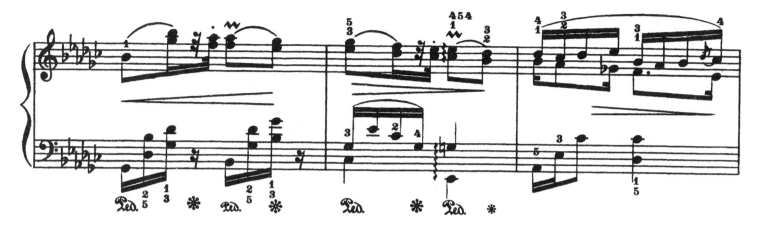

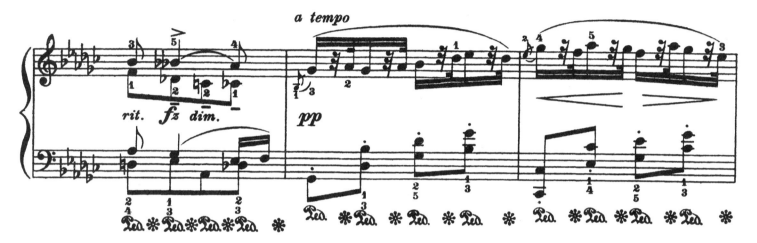

Nocturne
in C minor

John Field

to Rudolph Ganz

The White Peacock
from *Roman Sketches*

Charles T. Griffes
Op. 7, No. 1

Languidamente e molto rubato

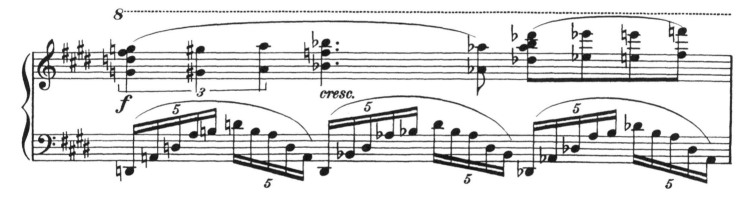

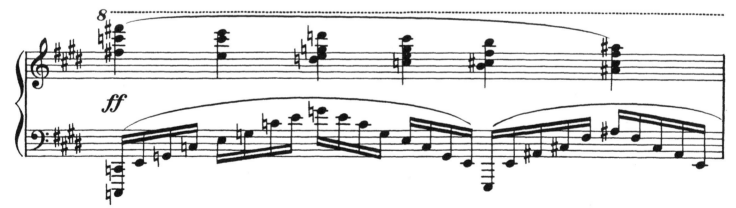

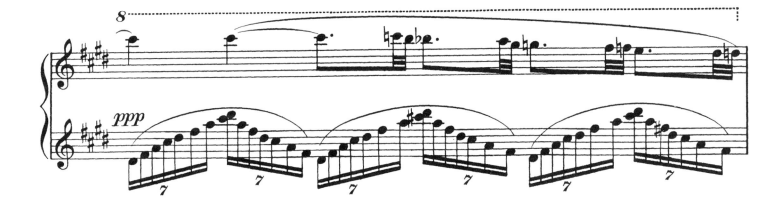

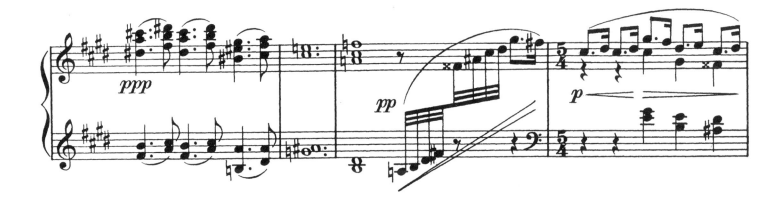

molto dim. e rit.

Wedding Day at Troldhaugen

from *Lyric Pieces*

Edvard Grieg
Op. 65, No. 6

Tempo di Marcia un poco vivace

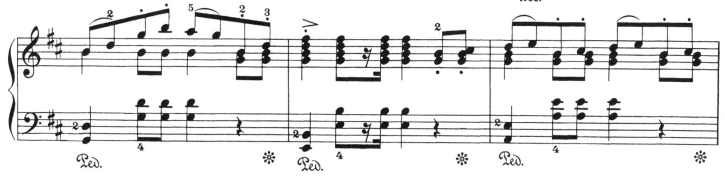

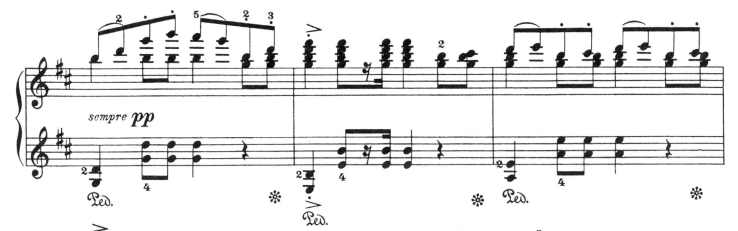

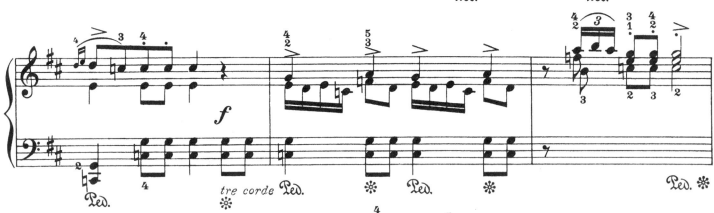

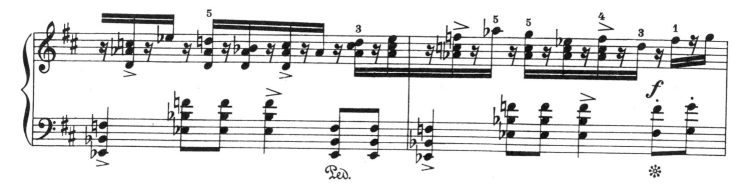

Tempo I

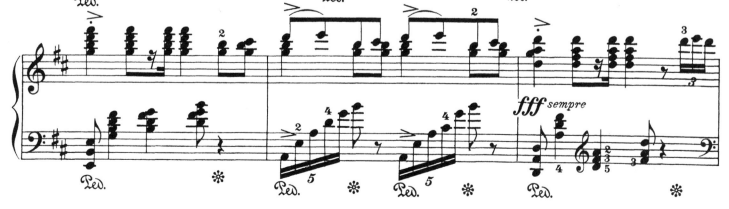

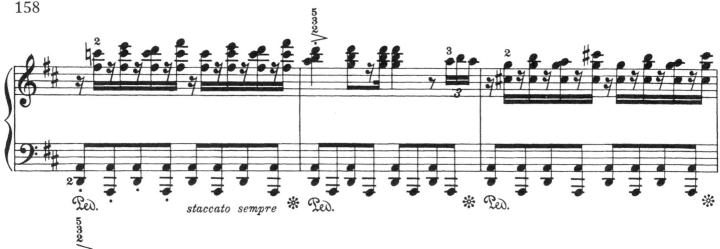

Liebestraum No. 3

from *Three Liebesträume: Three Notturnos*

Franz Liszt

Poco allegro, con affetto

poco cresc. ed agitato

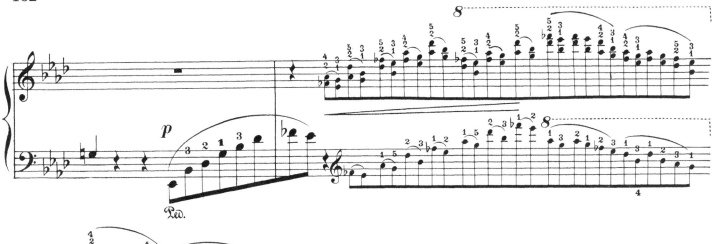

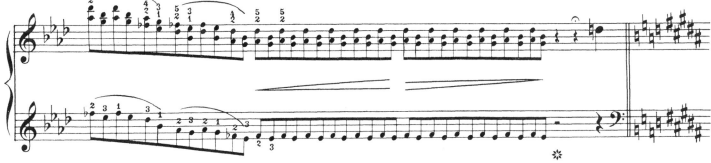

Più animato, con passione

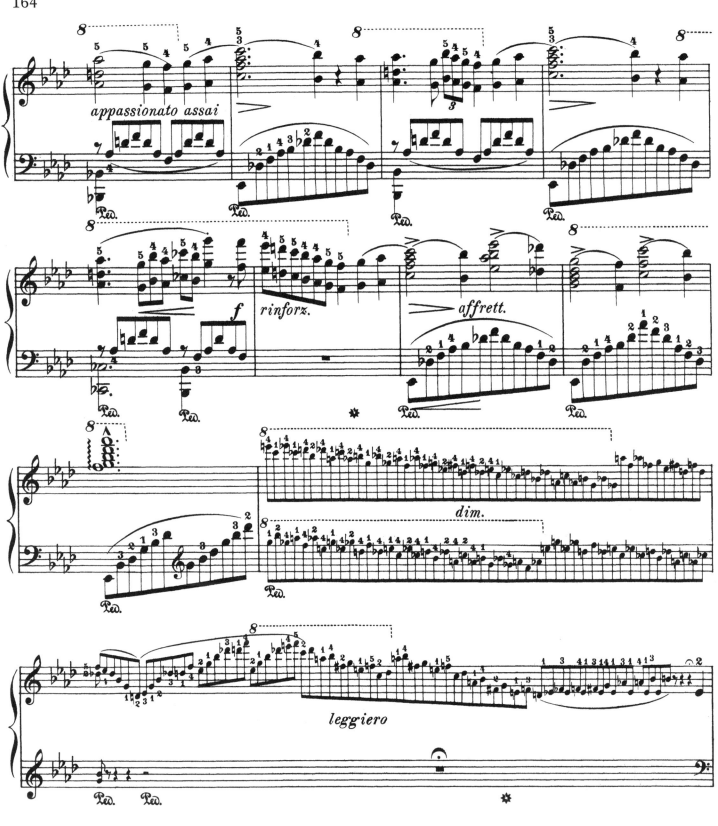

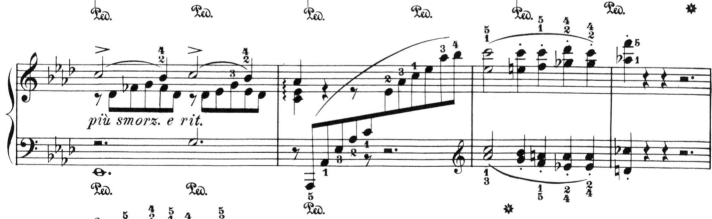

Il penseroso

from *Années de pèlerinage, Deuxiéme année: Italie*

Franz Liszt

Rondo capriccioso

Felix Mendelssohn
Op. 14

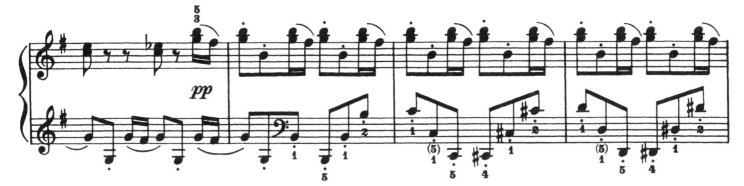

172

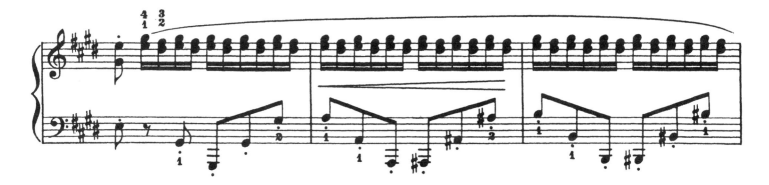

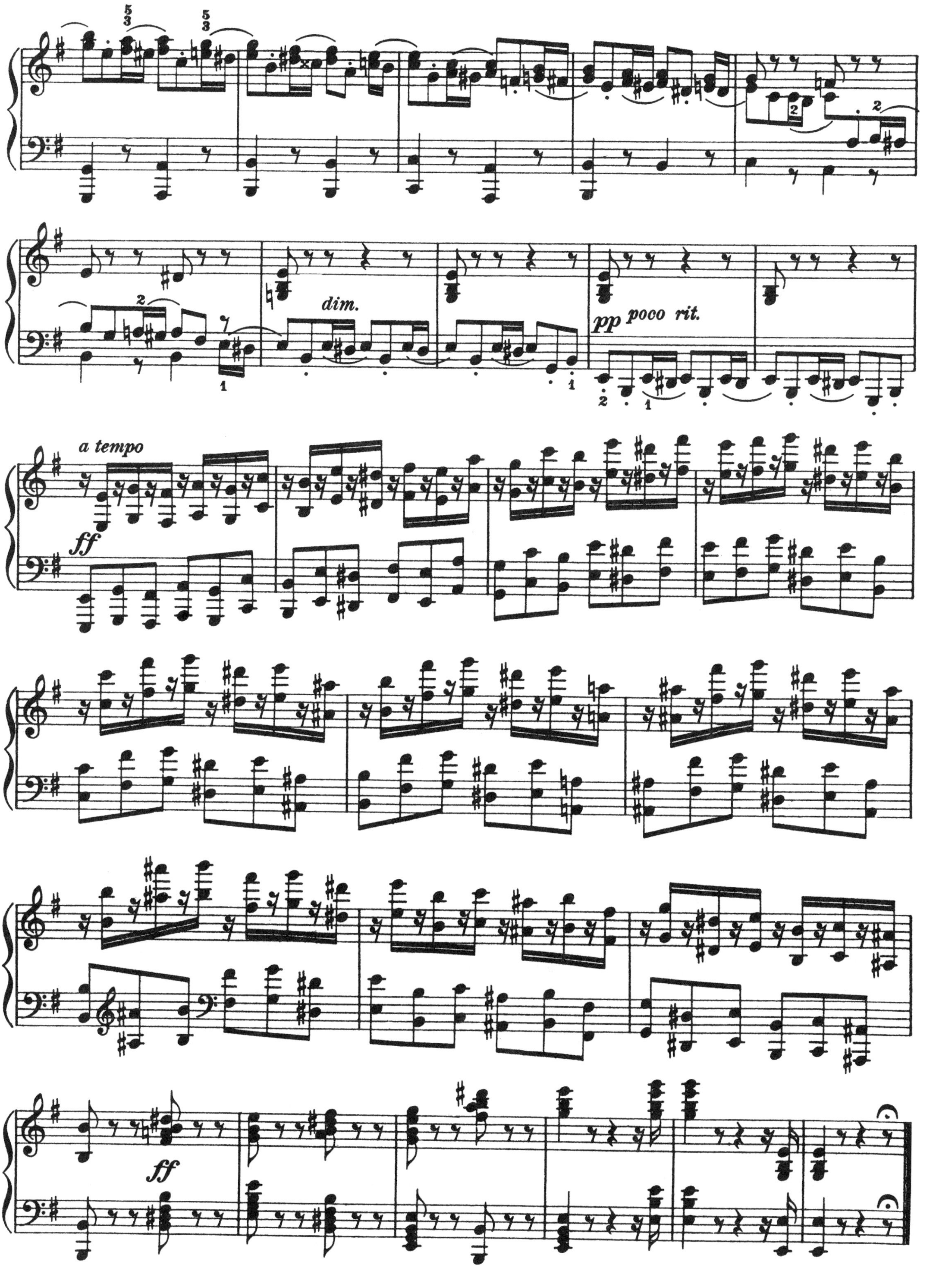
dim.
pp poco rit.
a tempo
ff
ff

Song Without Words
in A Major

Felix Mendelssohn
Op. 19, No. 3

Molto Allegro e vivace *)

Prelude
in G minor

Sergei Rachmaninoff
Op. 23, No. 5

Alla marcia ($\quad$=108)

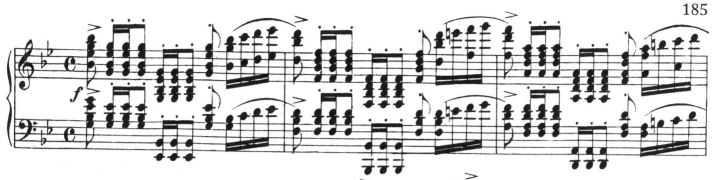

Un poco meno mosso

poco a poco accelerando e cresc. al Tempo I

Tempo I

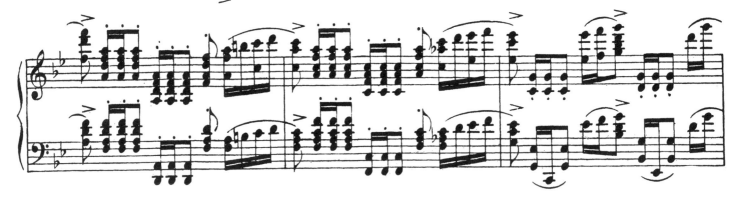

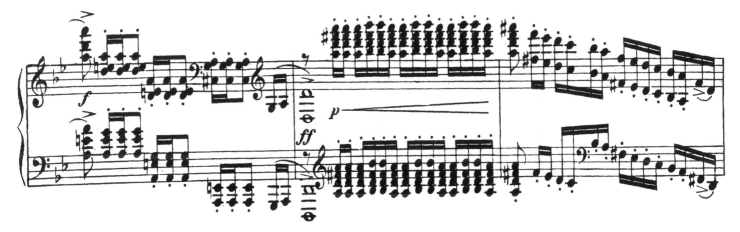

Prelude
in G Major

Sergei Rachmaninoff
Op. 32, No. 5

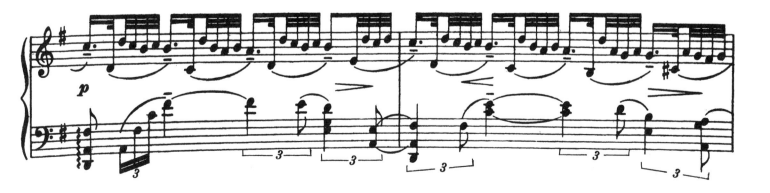

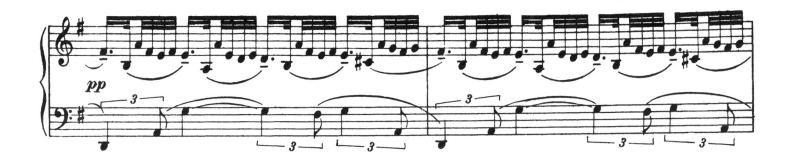

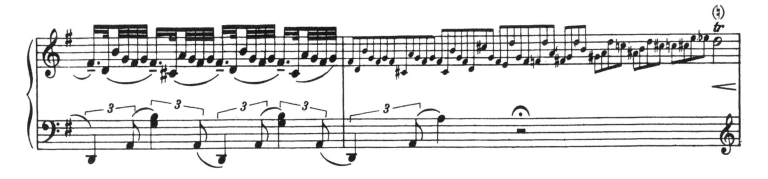

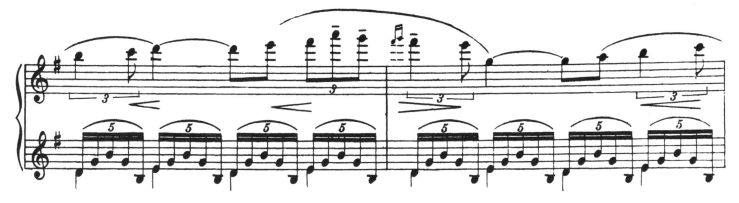

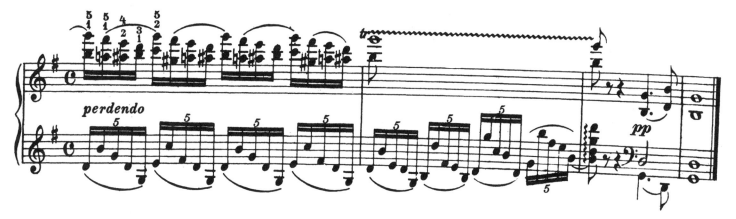

Piano Sonata
in D Major

Domenico Scarlatti
K. 96, L. 465

Allegrissimo

Mutandi i deti

Piano Sonata
in A Major

Domenico Scarlatti
K. 208, L. 238

Andante e cantabile

Moment musicaux
in C Major
from *Six moments musicaux*

Franz Schubert
Op. 94, No. 1

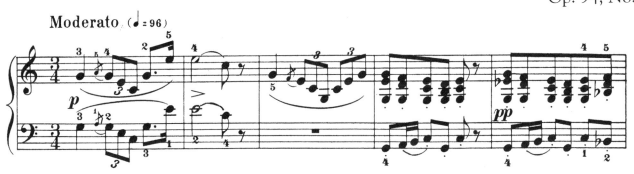

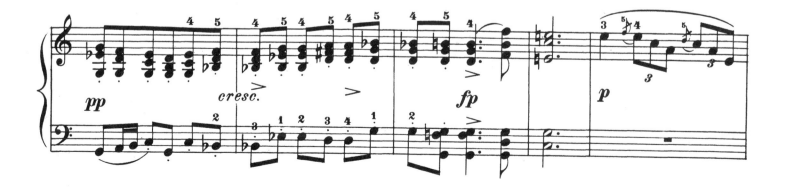

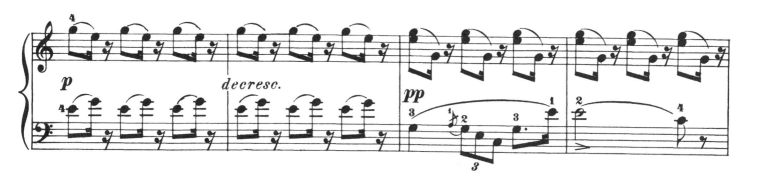

Impromptu
in G-flat Major
from *Four Impromptus*

Franz Schubert
Op. 90, No. 3

Andante mosso ($\quad$ = 84)

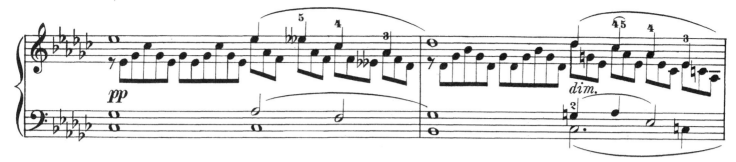

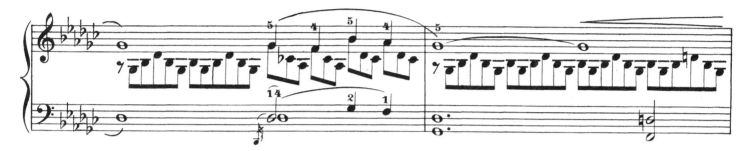

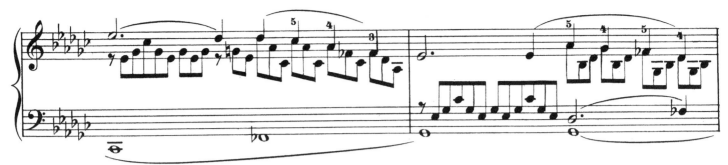

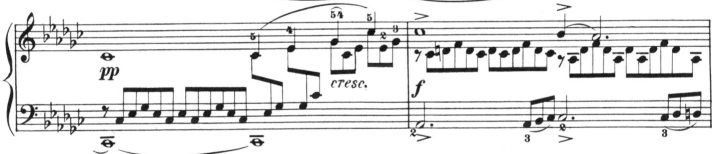

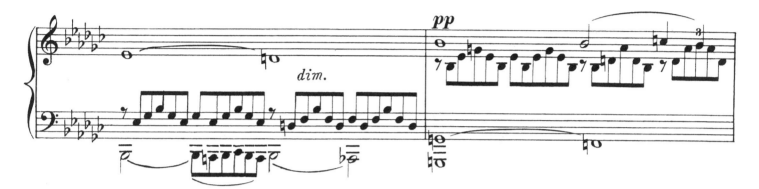

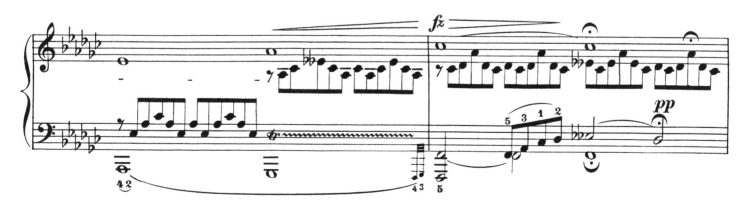

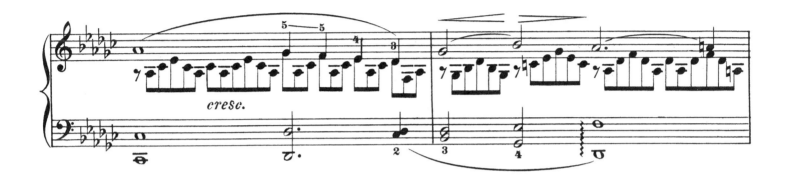

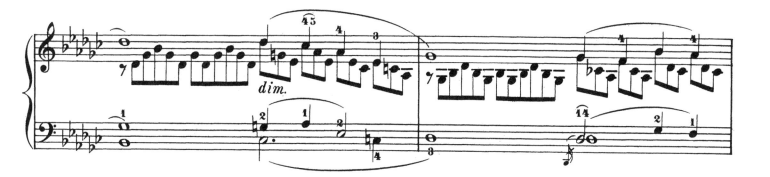

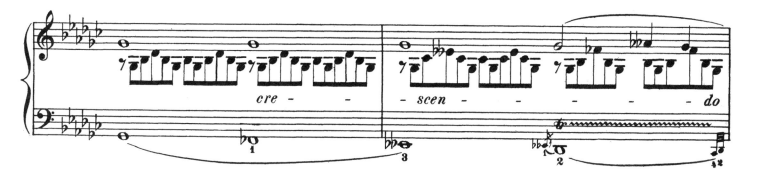

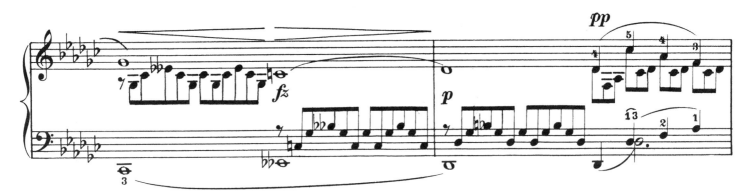

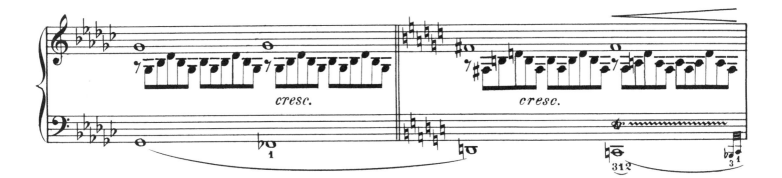

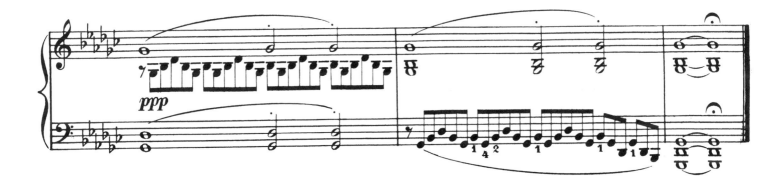

Vogel als Prophet

(The Bird as Prophet)

from *Forest Scenes*

Robert Schumann
Op. 82, No. 7

Aufschwung
(Soaring)
from *Fantasiestücke*

Robert Schumann
Op.12, No. 2

Warum?
(Why?)
from *Fantasiestücke*

Robert Schumann
Op. 12, No. 3

Chant sans paroles

from *Souvenir de Hapsal*

Pyotr Il'yrich Tchaikovsky
Op. 2, No. 3

Allegretto grazioso e cantabile.

Tempo I.

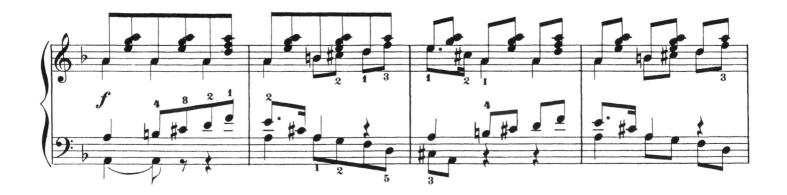

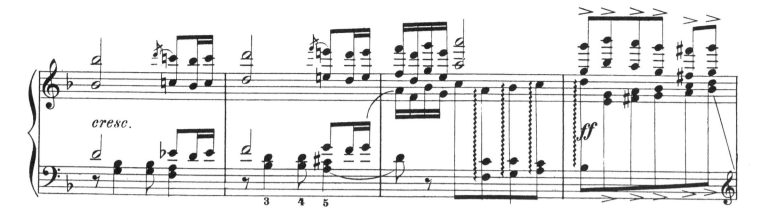

sempre di - mi -nu - en - do

marcata la melodia

Prelude
in A minor

Alexander Scriabin
Op. 11, No. 2

accel.   rit.

rit.

PRELUDE
in D-flat Major

Alexander Scriabin
Op. 11, No. 15

PRELUDE
in D-flat Major

Alexander Scriabin
Op. 11, No. 15